THE ACTUAL MOON, T

Other volumes in the series:

The Morse Poetry Prize
Edited by Guy Rotella

CHRIS FORHAN

The Actual Moon, The Actual Stars

THE 2003 MORSE
POETRY PRIZE
❧ SELECTED AND
INTRODUCED BY
ROBERT CORDING

*For Peter, with fondness &
admiration & with hopes that
our paths can meet again
often.*

Chris Forhan

December 2003

Northeastern University Press
BOSTON

Northeastern University Press

Copyright 2003 by Chris Forhan

Library of Congress Cataloging-in-Publication Data
Forhan, Chris, 1959–
    The actual moon, the actual stars / Chris Forhan.
       p. cm. — (The 2003 Morse Poetry Prize)
    ISBN 1-55553-594-1 (pbk. : alk. paper)
    I. Title. II. Morse Poetry Prize ; 2003.
    PS3556.O7316.64 2003
    811'.54—dc21   2003013886

Designed by Ann Twombly

Composed in Weiss. Printed and bound by Sheridan Books, Ann Arbor, Michigan. The paper is House Natural, an acid-free stock.

MANUFACTURED IN THE UNITED STATES OF AMERICA
07   06   05   04   03   5   4   3   2   1

for Liz

ACKNOWLEDGMENTS

Grateful acknowledgment is made to the editors of the following journals in which these poems first appeared.

Ascent:	"Pietà"
Bellingham Review:	"Erasure," "Quiet Hours," "The Past"
Boulevard:	"Some Words from My Ghost"
DoubleTake:	"Got No Blues"
88: A Journal of Contemporary American Poetry:	"Where the Past Went," "Deciduous," "In the Very Temple of Delight, Veil'd Melancholy," "It Couldn't Have Been Helped, It Was for the Best"
Georgia Review	"No Comment"
Gulf Coast:	"Sepia-Tinted" (under the title "In Sepia")
Hayden's Ferry Review:	"Sixteen"
Laurel Review:	"Names I've Been Called"
Nebraska Review:	"Keeping House Alone"
New England Review:	"Gouge, Adze, Rasp, Hammer," "My Gospel Is"
Parnassus:	"The Hard Sciences"
Ploughshares:	"The Actual Moon, The Actual Stars," "From a Shaded Porch," "Lonesome Tableau"
Poetry:	"Billet-Doux," "The Fidgeting," Late Winter Rain," "Nothing Doing"
Shenandoah:	"The Coast of Oklahoma"
Willow Springs:	"Dumbwaiter to Heaven"

"The Actual Moon, The Actual Stars," "The Fidgeting," "Gouge, Adze, Rasp, Hammer," and "Nothing Doing" were reprinted in *Hammer and Blaze: A Gathering of Contemporary American Poets* (University of Georgia Press).

"The Past" was reprinted in *The Pushcart Prize XXVII: Best of the Small Presses* 2003 (Pushcart Press).

"Gouge, Adze, Rasp, Hammer" was reprinted in *Poetry 180: A Turning Back to Poetry* (Random House).

"The Fidgeting" was reprinted in *The Book of Irish American Poetry from the Eighteenth Century to the Present* (University of Notre Dame Press).

Many friends and colleagues deserve thanks for assisting in the completion of the manuscript of this book: Charles Wright, Rita Dove, Gregory Orr, Laura Kasischke, the community of writers at the University of Virginia and Warren Wilson College, and my first, most generous, and most valued reader, Liz Green.

I am also grateful to the Yaddo artists' colony, where, over the course of two productive summers, many of these poems were written. Thanks as well to Guy Rotella for editorial advice on the book and to Robert Cording for choosing the manuscript.

Contents

III

Introduction

Chris Forhan borrows a line from John Keats—"Ay, in the very temple of Delight,/Veil'd Melancholy has her sovran shrine"—for one of his titles. The tip of the hat to Keats says much about the world of Chris Forhan's poetry, a world of paradox and contradictory impulses, a world that constantly requires Negative Capability to keep us from blotting out "the actual moon, the actual stars" with the imagination's "dove-winged blendings," as Wallace Stevens, another of Forhan's poetical forefathers, put it. Over and over again, these poems shape the tensions that arise from Stevens's "ever restless mind" and the world around us in which the mushroom's gills, the pip of the grape, the "council of birds" that peck at the dead fawn to clean its remains all simply do, without thought, what they do. Only the human speaker asks, "what is one to do" on a perfectly beautiful night when a fern "rooted at the road's edge/casts the shadow of an infant's ribs." "No Comment," the title of this collection's first poem, is Forhan's wonderfully wry answer; it acknowledges both that we cannot keep from asking such questions and that any answer we provide would only entangle us that much more.

Thankfully, Chris Forhan cannot hold his tongue, and in the poems that follow—often lit by a playful sense of humor and a voice that is truly engaging—he creates a landscape that is both intensely physical and replete with the age-old questions: is there something behind the change of seasons when the "world's furniture" is "suddenly in a new room" without our ever having detected any movement ("Nothing Doing"); is there something in our connection to the universe which, despite our best efforts to remain asleep, "flutter[s] one's eyelids open to a sudden wonder" ("December 1999"); if, to rephrase Stevens, death were not the mother of beauty, could we find beauty in the unchanging leaves on a tree, in azaleas that were only themselves and not an announcement of spring ("On an Old

Melodrama"); could we give up the "frail" forms we impose upon disorder ("The Actual Moon, The Actual Stars"); can we live without despair in the "baffling shadow" the past casts upon us ("The Past"); and is it our very human nature—our capacity to dream—that leads us into a life of contradictions ("Before")? Forhan's poetical self needs Negative Capability because he is always caught between oppositional tugs—between homelessness and stars that are guides or a home and stars that are forgotten and merely "pretty" ("Sepia-Tinted"); between being an "astonished infant" looking upon the physical world and a "fidgeting" adult who looks upon a "sodden collection/of fallen leaves blown against a fence" and finds it "wearisome" ("The Fidgeting"); between the sense that there is "some radiant unreason" that "the body took into itself/with fine inattention" and the fact that our language cannot express it ("Erasure").

But these poems know how, in Richard Wilbur's phrase, "to keep their difficult balance." Though they are always seeking understanding, always moving out toward the world rather than inward toward the self, they are also self-deprecating, quick-witted, and full of surprising turns. In one of my favorite poems, Forhan moves quickly from a set of literary figures who try to measure the proper dose of happiness, to the fact that they came to misery, to himself lounging outside in a plastic chair with a beer enjoying the warmth of summer. Winter is gone; the only "dark touch" in a landscape of color is a crow sitting on a fence post, and the speaker, listening to the hammering up the street, enjoying the order of a green garden hose coiled on the toolshed, finds himself "compelled to forgive/my little cruelties toward myself and others." But though he simply enjoyed that moment in the afternoon, he cannot help wondering later that night what he would have said about the "warmth of the backyard," now a fading memory. Here's the end of the poem ("The Very Button"):

> . . . I am only remembering the warmth of the backyard
> that needed, at the time, no explication, though if pressed
> to utter some words on the occasion—

if the neighbor kid, say, held a squirt gun to my head
and all the swallows stopped their song and settled
on the tips of branches
and cocked their little heads toward me—

I might have said
on Fortune's cap we are the very button.

At their best, Chris Forhan's poems have a jester's wisdom. Throughout *The Actual Moon, The Actual Stars*, the reader follows a trustworthy guide who is always led by Tolstoy's great question: How then shall we live? Though Chris Forhan does not presume to answer, he lives the question, as Rilke advised, in all its complexity. And, in doing so, his warm, wise, and inventive poems help us to come face-to-face with a world that is "incoherent," "addressed to no one," but "therefore useless and beautiful." They deserve the last word:

Summary and Invocation

The moon mouthing its own name,
the stars tracing on the sky's slate all night,
the lake in a trance,
the sudden heavy rain that believes in the laying on of hands,
and the finch in the jack pine.

The wind fumbling at everything's buttons,
the brook working to tie itself into a half-hitch,
the June peaks tipped with snow, a pentimento of winter—
part of the world's incoherent letter, addressed to no one,
     therefore useless and beautiful.
And the finch in the jack pine.

ROBERT CORDING

This mangled, smutted semi-world hacked out

Of dirt . . . It is not possible for the moon
To blot this with its dove-winged blendings.

—WALLACE STEVENS

I

No Comment

In the leaf's veins and midrib,
the mushroom's gill: no irony.

In the stamen and pistil,
the pip of the grape, making

occurs without suffering,
one is led to suppose.

When the fawn sprawled in a thicket
stiffens, a council of birds

descends and pecks
until its chest is crimson.

The badger's project
is isolation: he knows

only to burrow and sleep,
while the spider spins

in a web wider, more intricate
than his, though this crisis

does not cross his mind.
He proceeds without comment.

Then what is one to do
on a night like this, bright almost

as day, when the lavender moon,
burdened with light,

is near enough to brush
the trees and power lines, when this fern

rooted at the road's edge
casts the shadow of an infant's ribs?

Nothing Doing

Stub of December, the year in a fast fade.
Christmas trees dragged stump-first to the curb,
clumps of wrinkled tinsel the only glitter.

All else—grass, sky—dead yellow,
all else wan and resigned, the black, burnt-out
wick of the year too weak to raise a flame.

Everything looking a little late and left behind:
power line slumped and swinging in a stiff breeze,
wheelchair abandoned beneath the off-ramp,

two-by-four moldering in a ditch, its single
bent nail like a rusty finger bone.
Grackle perched on a mailbox, staring

at nothing. He's right to take a hard look.
I always miss it, too: the turn, the wheeze
of one year becoming the whispered

intimation of a new one, the world's furniture
suddenly in a new room without moving.
It's now, with strict attention, one might

detect the mechanism: the webbed intricacy
of the grackle's brain, the planets stirring up
their circles of dust. Perhaps it's now we're nearest

to something that could save us—something
beyond our knowledge and our will to believe it.
The day is stark, hushed, ground down

to particulars, as if encrypted.
Time to watch for a sign, a shift. When
nothing happens, I'll have my proof.

December 1999

So. Bloated moon. There it is. I didn't miss it.
Biggest in 133 years, the newspaper says.
Something about the poles of the earth—
their direction, something about the winter solstice.
I'm walking toward a restaurant with a woman
of whom I knew nothing when last the moon was full.
Of this moon, I know its plumpness is a trick—
so, too, the way it shines like a new-minted nickel:
old moon, evoker of platitudes, assuming its role
in a new illusion. Anyone with time and a telescope
might have seen this coming. It has to do
with the orbit of bodies in space, the earth's
location relative to the moon and sun.
The red alder's leaves hang glossy, lacquered
in this light. They do not rustle. The breeze
and even the closest, most radiant star
dawdle offstage. Tonight, the corpulent moon
goes solo: it squats and waits to be pondered.
In ten days, the odometer of the big Christian car
we ride in will show an imposing row of zeroes.
It's hard to keep one's eyes on the road
with such a thing coming—a distracted glance away
and one could miss it. It's hard not to think
of how any moment is fugitive—hollow,
then gone—but how, as it makes its long approach,
it holds every possible cargo: every gladness
and ruin imaginable. Tonight, the moon is a zero,
a fat blank: silver, with hints of blue, though this, too,
is only a trick of perspective. I'm walking
with a woman of whose thousand stories and one
I know but two or three, though I know my stories well;
my heart tugs at my sleeve, pleading to tell

its favorite already. Gravity is involved,
of course: the moon hauled along by the earth
as it circles nearer than usual to the sun.
Timing, also—this being one of those nights
the moon steps out from behind the curtain
of the earth's shadow. I'm feeling a little obvious
myself tonight, I'm feeling prone to overstatement.
I'm walking beneath an improbable moon
with a woman whose name will soon keep me up late
racking my skull for rhymes. There's something about
convergence going on, something about the turning of objects
and seasons and about the position of things
in relation to each other, for which there are laws,
so it is possible to live as if dead a long time
then flutter one's eyelids open to a sudden wonder
that might have been expected
had one thought harder about how bodies
rotate in space on invisible tethers, about the role
of natural law—about how, being a law, it is followed.

Billet-Doux

She reads by the light of a guttering candle
and likes the feel of each page's gilt edge
as she lifts it slightly at the corner, readying

herself to turn it. If the wind whips
the sycamore branches outside her window,
if her nightgowned shoulders shudder once

from a sudden chill, so much the better,
and the book must tell of children toiling
for bread and pennies in a textile mill,

or tender brothers doomed to sharpen
their bayonets in opposing armies,
or a family of refugees, dust

in their mouths, gazing with longing at the far
shore of a river. And I long only
to be the author of that book she reads

whose page glows from the same dim
flame that illuminates her face,
the author whose thought she contemplates

as she touches a fingertip to a word
to mark her place and turns her head
toward the kettle that has begun to whistle.

On an Old Melodrama

There's too much talk of you, Persephone,
sucked down into your late November sewer grate,
spit back in April to stumble

dazed, half-dressed, among us, making your way
to your mother's rose garden
so you can faint, weeping, into her arms.

Hokum like that—what ice-packed heart
wouldn't thaw, what bad poet
wouldn't lick his pencil tip?

Because we miss you and you return,
the days of June seem long, December
a cheat. Because of you, our teeth

rip the flesh of the ripe peach
too eagerly: we recall
the dark, how we bargained for a crust

of the stalest bread. O Persephone,
stay home for good this time.
Ditch the creep. Lose the crazy accent.

Use the local slang like the rest of the girls
until we think of you—if we do at all—
as nothing special, *Princess Whoozits, What's-Her-Face.*

Let one month yield to the next unnoticed
and the leaves remain on the tree
and the birds repeat their song till it's only chatter.

For once, let us see the flaming azalea
for what it is, though it disappoint.
For once, let summer earn our love.

The Very Button

It is too much of joy, said the Moor. That's a point.
Perhaps the brightest diamond of bliss
comes bundled in the black cloth of our knowledge
of what it would mean to lose it. But who would choose
Heathcliff's way: *Too happy, and yet not happy enough,*
or throw one's lot in with noncommittal, just-this-side-of-thoughtful
Guildenstern: *Happy* in being *not over-happy.* Oh

measure as they may, all three
came to misery, as soon this bee will who now
is immersed in work, his reconnaissance among the dahlias,
while I lounge in the backyard in a plastic chair
with a pint of beer, the height of summer.

Clumsy world, clumsy me, I'm given to say,
though all day for no discernible reason
I've carried myself with delicacy
like a tray of crystal goblets, wine
wobbling at the brim. Of winter, what remains is only
a thin hoard of thoughts, my mind's platonic January,
a winter of symbols: man in coat and galoshes,
romping dog rolling in snow, leafless tree
a shape scissored from sky.

                              Today a lone crow,
quick black stroke on a fence post, is the one dark touch
that deepens the composition's color: the too blue, boundless sky,
   the green
garden hose coiled, hanging on the toolshed, the bright red
hammering from the half-finished house up the street.

Suddenly, I'm compelled to forgive
my little cruelties toward myself and others,
to forget my daily litany of desires

denied or granted. I feel moved
to write no poem, not even this one, which, truth be told,

had to wait for a time less tranquil
to worry itself into being. I am sitting, I admit,
at a metal desk now. It is night.
The air is a little chilly for my liking
and my cup of coffee has cooled too quickly

and I am only remembering the warmth of the backyard
that needed, at the time, no explication, though if pressed
to utter some words on the occasion—
if the neighbor kid, say, held a squirt gun to my head
and all the swallows stopped their song and settled
on the tips of branches
and cocked their little heads toward me—

I might have said
on Fortune's cap we are the very button.

From a Shaded Porch

Mid-August. Crippling heat. Torpor.
Lungs weighed down by the stubborn air.
Sudden, hyperbolic, dog-startling storms

each afternoon, uninspired repertoire
of kettle- and window-rattling.
Who'd settle for an arrangement like this?

Who wouldn't? Too hot to do otherwise. Hard
to think twice or overachieve in such weather.
One is compelled to be dumb, to slump

on the porch until the season's gone, speaking
only now and again out of boredom,
abandoning sentences halfway through,

having forgotten their point. An old
pickup truck stutters by. Bad tail pipe.
Someone has to be somewhere.

Otherwise, hard to imagine moving.
Hard to conceive of packing the kids up
to cruise Route 82 and tour

the waxworks or roam the curiosity shop,
with its mummified Mayan princess,
pictures of bearded babies,

and prayers on a pinhead. Instead,
one sprawls, pleased to be stupid,
musing with approval

on the small, dark place between
the grass blades, on the potato bug
barely there beneath his cool stone.

The Hard Sciences

Whatever the mole thinks, I don't want to know.
Whatever is under the raccoon's mask,
whatever the rhododendron is selling—

its splash of white and rosy-purple
proof of some occult transaction
beneath the dampened soil: forget it.

And I won't starve or lose my way
hoping to stumble on God in the desert
or the dull, myth-charged dark of woods.

Instead, today I'm astonished
by the cloverleaf interchange—its functional
elegance. I'm charmed by the way

the railroad crossing arm's counterweight
works without a wasted ounce. I love
the shank of the anchor, the harvester's teeth

and auger, and how the crescent wrench
fits in my fist at one end, while the other
slips snugly around the bolt.

I might just stay up late tonight
crouched behind the dryer with my
Great Big Book of Home Repair,

letting the moon float by unnoticed
and knit his disapproving brow.
What use is the moon or Cassiopeia,

why connect Orion's dots
or muse upon the burning silence
of Mars or the Big and Little Dippers

unless by that we mean this ladle
that even now lowers an exquisite
crawfish bisque into my bowl

and this spoon, crafted exactly to match
the measure and contour of my desire,
that lifts it, steaming, to my mouth.

Confession

I was false to you, I admit,
when I clicked the radio off
as I drove alone to the hardware store
and gave my ardor over to the sure
seductions of your voice—it was not
you I wanted, not even your voice,
only the project of reconstructing
its music in all that traffic,
in the odd quiet of the car,
in the dark rehearsal hall of my skull.
I pondered the way your syllables
leap and skitter to follow
a nimble thought, and the way
you go suddenly silent, letting
a last word curl
and linger low to the ground
like smoke in rain. That morning
I needed a packing retainer ring
and washer for the bathroom faucet.
I did not need you, I thought—
only the allurement of memory
and imagination. It was a venial sin,
as this one is—

acting as though I could fill a hush, the nothing
of your not being here, with something
true to you, of my own making.
What was it this time, anyway?
Leap and skitter? Smoke in rain?

Late Meditation

Night again, and I'm not impressed:
the blurred cedar, blowzy in her black dress,
the bat's manic acrobatics—he tries too hard—
the hooligan raccoon routing in the brush,
and above all this the familiar, gaudy
glitter of the stars. Once I felt invited
to praise these things. Once I felt obliged.
Inviolable night, I said. *Love's rustling curtain.*
My hornbook, my slow ship to stow away on.
It took a long time to discover night
is a slate one writes on with the chalk
of desire. Look. The moon is thin as a dime.
It goes, and the sun comes up shrunken, low,
something to poke with a broom
and plunk, hissing, into a water bucket.
What I said, I'd like to take it back.

Late Winter Rain

Wind-wrenched pines, tantrum of rain
on the blacktop, flooded gutter aswirl
with sticks and paper cups—

thwarted desire in a riot—

late winter writhing with no body,
pummeling the air with no fists, importuning
without a tongue. For too long

a man remembers a woman

till her name is a nail driven
through the back of his mind, and he thinks it wise
not to speak of her, and her body

blurs, a confusion of shapes in shadow,

and the voice that sings in his head
isn't hers and is, and the face he loves
slips in and out of focus

like his own face, like the stranger's in the mirror

he shrinks from, watching sudden rain instead
spatter the walk, wind hurl itself blindly against a bush—
March, for weeks so tedious, so sensible,

beginning to make a fool of itself.

Lonesome Tableau

Tacked on the wall, a map of my sad luck,
places self-pity has planted its flag.
In the bed, my body, a book in its hand.

In my skull, a voice reciting the words
on the page one moment—an exegesis
of a bungled kiss—and then the next

enumerating the canyons and cliffs, the familiar
indigenous flowers and patterns of weather,
in the vast mapped reaches of my despair.

There are things it is best not to speak out loud:
deepest being, conscience of God,
though sometimes one desires to read them

in a book, then set the book down while the mind
wends it way around a sentence's sense,
but the mind is sorrow's topographer—

it wants as well to ponder the sheer
slopes on the map. It flatters itself
that its talent is being two places at once

when it hasn't the will to be anywhere at all
for long—certainly not in this book
I cannot finish, so thick, so difficult,

with its flashbacks, its too many women and men,
each attached to a hope, an intention.
In every room of my house, the same

distracting map of my own lost chances
but thousands of books to choose from. Perhaps
it's time for the tale of a ghost ship, timbers

groaning as it drifts with cracked mast
and tattered sail for months on the open sea.
Perhaps it's time for a poem with no people in it.

The Actual Moon, The Actual Stars

In that hour of boundless night when dark
tugs at me with its bustle and fuss

and the grass outside my window, gone
a deep blue, chirrs and clicks with crickets

and my thoughts flop and twitch
like fish in a galvanized bucket

and sweat soaks the sheets, collecting
in drops down my spine and behind my knees,

I like to leave my bones and flesh
lying in the bed while I roam the neighborhood,

only my being, the big idea of myself,
out for a stroll. I go undetected

by the sensor light in the side yard
and any dog or possum that crosses my path.

I go past the parked cars and clusters
of mailboxes, houses hunkered down

in the dark, an occasional light
whitening a single window. I go

without breath or breathlessness, I go
with forgiveness in my invisible heart

for the frail forms imposed upon
disorder: the painted stones a neighbor

has bordered his yard with, the black
plastic garbage bins

wheeled to the ends of driveways. I let
my mind forget its wrestling match

with the flesh, its urge to account for the burden
of the body by making of it an allegory.

I let whatever story I'm in
unfold its plot without interruption,

though chances are it is not a tale
about my welfare, and I cannot say

I comprehend what the least part of it
means, the bits of gravel scattered

on the blacktop glinting like stars, the battered
bottle cap glowing like a small fallen moon—

above, the actual moon, the actual stars
shining like nothing but themselves.

Pastoral

Where weeds wind around the junked car's axle, its trunk rusted,
  rat-inhabited—I could live there,
I could nod assent to the cedar waxwing's incoherent homily,

Now that my ruminating has gone awry, now that my heart's full
  of waste and leavings, I could live there,
Where the rabbit hustles into the thicket and the cricket sings one
  thing all night,

Where the spruce droops one day then writhes in the wind the
  next, like a heretic at the stake,
With my burnt brain, my stuck tongue,

Among the abandoned paint cans and baling wire, the fallen tool-
  shed's rotting wood, I could live
Sworn to silence, with my hat of dandelions, my beard of bees.

II

Before

The moon and constellations were not then.
Nor tides, horizons, graves—all was ocean,
and we lived on the great whale's back,
a whale so vast in none of our roaming
did we once behold its head or tail.
The air hummed with light. The sky
was a flat, unchanging white, the white
of the sea. The practice of women
was to pin a sprig of berries in their hair
and of men to loop a blade of grass
around their wrists. But not for luck, not for beauty.
Luck was not then. Beauty was not then.
We did not choose between the weed and the rose.
We let the bee rest in our palm,
the scorpion ride on our shoulders.
Then one of us slept and dreamed fire,
and there was fire, and with it
the first brief dark and chill. Another
dreamed stars, and there were stars, and some of us
were stunned by this into silence, some
into song. That was the first singing.
Somebody, fluttering his eyes shut, swooned
and changed his face to the shade of ash.
One of us laughed. That was the first laugh.
For some time, the man who had fallen
was understood to be dreaming.

Sepia-Tinted

Through flooded fields, up hills and rivers, down
mountains in mud so deep our cart wheels
stuck and splintered, at last our travels

brought us by chance to an unnamed tributary
and this town, this outpost we knew first only
as a far column of smoke over pine tops,

and the people received us and fed us, and though
their language was strange, as ours was to them,
the roads were cobbled and the dogs were tame,

and we knew by the third day we would stay,
and we burned our foul clothes: doused them with fuel,
forgot them in a rush of flame, and pried apart

our wagons for paling fences, raised walls, tarred roofs,
and told each other this was the life we had dreamed of
through weeks of rowing, months of hard portage,

and then we said less and less, and this was a comfort,
and as for the stars that had been our guides, we forgot their names
but agreed they were pretty, and we dimmed the town lamps

to give them a look, and we lit our halls with candle flames
that stuttered and bent back as we passed,
which was sad, though we could not say why,

so we took to sitting still and thinking, depending
for company on the voice in our heads, which seemed a stranger's,
and our children grew tall in their little rooms

and we did not tell them the story of our travels
because it was no longer ours, although in sleep
our shoulders ached, and our old boats warped on the shore.

What's Left

The way the country squire's vast pastureland
is alluded to
in each yard's little polygon of lawn

is like the way the lawn is rhymed by
carpet nailed from one horizon of a room to another
so, stepping upon it, a body recalls
something of long-gone summers
when lovers, it's said, might wander together
all morning in glens and meadows
and meet no one else,

though now the nearest flowers
are scissor-clipped, set upright
on the mantel—or stamped in patterns
on daisy-print curtains in the kitchen—

and since, in the misty past, someone
plunged into a pond,
we spray the bath with lavender and lie
back in the tub with eyes closed

while the dank cellar holds
sealed boxes so old
we've forgotten what's in them.

Grave Robbing by Daylight

Still in sleep's big coat, I slip through the back gate
into the morning drizzle. My black umbrella
ratchets open like a claw, a horror movie prop.

A thought has half-awoken me: the past is in pieces,
scattered, buried, but recoverable—so are the laws
of its long, exacting operations, so is the heart

that throbbed within me once. In the alley
where blackberry bushes grew wild for years
before they were bulldozed under, I smell again

their sweet, immodest ripeness, cut with the heat
and dust of summer. I cross the edge of the park
where on a Sunday evening when I was nine I spied

my trumpet teacher, alone on a bench, munching a pear.
He's there—the fruit, half-eaten, still in his hand.
Each street appears before me like the line of a story

I erase as I go. There, before it was gutted,
remade as a Christian Science Reading Room,
was Rummond's Hardware—I smell it still,

the grease, the burlap sacks packed with nails. My bike
hit a patch of gravel here and flipped me into a ditch.
There I found a dollar bill on the sidewalk.

That girl in the drugstore window, eyes scrunched shut,
tongue stuck out, could be my little sister.
But I am nowhere. Scraps of what I saw,

not was. Pieces that can't be pieced together.
Where is the simple self I've heard of, me before memory,
blank book the blur of days scrawled its name on—

unless, in that vacant lot, where a man
leans on a shovel, smoke billowing black from an upright barrel—
unless that's me feeding the flames.

Names I've Been Called

Pike-Eyed Pickle-Head. Saddle-Backed Weeper.
Whenever Father and Mother agreed
on a name for me in my early years,

I'd change. They'd have to choose another.
Whistling Rufus. Frog of October.
Quiet Sidekick. Box of Luck.

When someone called me in to supper,
part of me answered. Always it was this way,
taking on a name like an ill-fitting garment,

burdened by obedience to the world outside,
which made its kind of sense, and to
the blank map within, which made another.

Recumbent in Summer, Father asked,
how is your leek soufflé? Mmm, good,
I answered. It felt like a lie.

At twelve, for weeks I moped in my room.
No name moved me. The house grew cold.
Outside my window, the moon burned.

At last, I entered my parents' bedroom
begging. How could they ever know me
enough—a boy unknown to himself?

Stop, I pleaded. Call me nothing,
or call me son. Mother squeezed my hand. Oh,
she whispered. Oh, *Long Gone Long Gone* . . .

For Now

Fourteen, suburban, full of waffles, I loll
in a blue plastic and aluminum lawn chair.
Saturday morning. My chore: clean the toolshed.

I'll lug it all—lawn mower, ladder, sack
of roofing nails, cans of varnish, goggles,
gardening gloves—onto the sunlit patio.

But for now
I'm watching slack in the clothesline,
a slight, exact
sinking in the middle. The sky
is white and scuffed, like a baseball,
and a bird flits beneath the plum tree
among the fallen, split fruit, tasting
one, then another.

My mother is done with the breakfast dishes.
She's scrubbing the kitchen window, eyeing me.
She's picking at something on the glass with a fingernail.

I'll sweep the shed.
I'll take a soapy rag to the metal shelves,
chisel the black splotch of paint from the bottom one,
then line the shelves again
with cans of motor oil, window putty, slug bait.

For now, though, I'm sitting,
something budging in me.
I'm deciding I need to keep an eye
on the slatted fence, its swaying set
of diamonds—shadow cast
by the basketball hoop's frayed net.

Maybe I think the shed will clean itself.

Maybe I'm on the verge of believing
there are words

for the leaf of the rhododendron, bent
from the weight of a snail at its tip,
for the squirrel that's leapt
to the lip of the birdbath
and hunkers, paws to chin,
as if in prayer. I think

I would sing the words, not say them.

Maybe I know
everything is in its place
and I am too, and the best attention
is wholly purposeless, wholly secret,
although it is not unlike
love—it is a kind of love—
and my mother, too, is right:
I'm just sitting here.

It Rusts Iron and Ripens Corn

Time to rub wax paper on the playground slide—
bring its slipperiness back—
now that June's here, time to oil the swing,
to think of what's gone
from the robin's egg that I plucked
from the tall weeds—a blue so pale, so delicate
that the shell, as it rests on the sill
of my window, seems hardly here.

And the egg says: Let go.
And sleep says: There's something you're forgetting, think again.
And the pond water says: Not so fast.
And the sky says: Nothing nothing nothing.
And the long swaying grass says: Dillydally.
And the frog says: Change.
And the rust specks on the slide say: Silence soon.
And the robin says: Soon, not now, not yet.

The Past

How worthy of attention, the past. How much less
predictable than the present, all bluster and disarray—

rugs tumbling from open truck beds, roof and joist rot,
loose dogs and wind. The future is barren: white, odorless.

But what of the scent when Grandpa worked the cider press
years ago? That meant something. How much sweeter

the scent has grown. It seems to have lingered for weeks,
rising from the cellar, gathering in every room.

What of the year of the barley market downturn? The year
Joe Wilkey took to drink? Not so awful, really.

Every dawn, in memory, offers its drawn-out vowel
of possibility, each sunset steeps us

in deep burgundy and pink. The bedroom fire, the loss
of half the house, seems a small thing now,

though occasions of elation—the day
the aircraft carrier nuzzled the waves as it entered

the bay, or that youthful escapade
involving the slowly sinking rubber raft—

seem intricate and grim. They loom
like a gray, rain-drenched monument.

The spring of the trolley operators' strike—
when Father bought the Rambler—puzzles. Why recall it

with such clarity? Whatever we were going to be
is back there still, a bird flittering through a scraggly wood.

How small the desire we quell, indiscriminately licking
the swizzle stick of the present, when there's the past

to think of: how it casts its baffling shadow upon us,
how it goes on forever, and holds such promise.

Sixteen

I would have trapped dawn
in a trash bin, lured the robin
to a closet and locked it in,
ripped up by the roots
a bush of fat blackberries—gorged,
like me, on their own hearts' juices.
I would have stained my fingers with them.

I wanted something
and couldn't say what it was
though I was darkly in love with a girl,
or maybe two, and my brain played
one song over and over, something
I'd found on a B-side,
slow and quarrelsome.

I pressed an ear to the wall—
muffled clatter of the family
gathering for dinner—then slunk
from the house, wool cap pulled low.
Well, whatever, I thought, glancing
at the maple waving its thousand hands.
I walked and walked, until my misery

stuck to me like rain-soaked clothes
and became a kind of happiness
and I crouched to watch a purple swirl
of oil in a ditch. From a weedy thicket
a flurry of birds flapped up, scattering
across the blank of the sky.
It felt like my idea.

It Couldn't Have Been Helped, It Was for the Best

When the loved one, lost, lives at last
only in memory, no longer in the frenzy
of one's wish that the film rewind on the reel
and breath blow back
and the snake repeal its bite;

When one has mourned, then chosen
to mourn, then been distracted out of mourning;

When one has forgiven oneself the disconsolate songs
that seemed, upon reflection,
a thoughtless flaunting of the self;

When one has almost forgotten
the doomed excursion beneath grief's theater:
the reckless mission of rescue into the cellarage,
the backward glance that only made the lost love
lost again,

        and one has gone on living
till hardly a cell in the body is left that knows
how one wept
for the stopped heart to stutter and pump again;

When one has come to feel
it is a comfort simply to sit still
within the fading days
and watch the vast shadow of evening reach
the farthest edge of the yard, like a lid slid shut—

Why wouldn't he press his palms against his ears
amid the whispers
about how winter's wail was merely a false alarm,
how spring's big promise is scenting the air with strawberry
and setting sprinklers on the lawn,
how the stone has rolled from the tomb?

Pietà

It's good that the sky today is like slate,
that the wind off the lake is cold

and the doorways of the shops on Main Street
are cast in shadow. It's easy now

to feel put upon, sullen. It's easy for everyone
to trudge through the city alone

carrying his own Christ in his arms:
a small Christ, the size of a cocker spaniel,

but real—unfastened, lowered from his pole,
looking a little flesh-burdened still,

with pale, blood-streaked brow and hanging limbs,
though burnished, aglow, lit from within.

One man holds his Christ to his chest
with both arms, as if cradling a baby

or grocery bag. Another has his swung
over his shoulder like a cement sack.

Two or three carry their Christ
stiffly before them with outstretched arms

as if holding a bundle for a stranger
tying his shoe. But no one lets go.

It's good to own your own version
of a big hurt, to contemplate the weight of it,

the bits of dried blood it leaves on your shirt
like flecks of rust. It's good to lug

an imponderable sadness, to touch its cool flesh
and gaze at its face: at the look an old master

could only approximate—the expression
you could never put into words,

not even for the lover aching to know you,
not even if you wanted to.

Here

In the neighboring county, night arrives
with light luggage, begging pardon, just
passing through. The sun hums itself up
then lingers on church towers
until it is roundly applauded.
Here we wake to wind
worrying the vents, to a cloud-clotted sky
of shifting grays, the implications of which
we spend all day considering.
In that other county, wasps have forgotten
to sting, bread to go stale. Children
in pastel sweaters, like wedding mints,
pause at brook-sides so swans
might nibble cake from their cupped palms.
Our kids titter in the crooks of branches,
thin legs dangling, or cluster
at the schoolyard fence to lob
clods of dirt at passing hearses.
There, no mood bruises; no thought
is darkened by desire or a sense
of one season surrendering to the next.
All week—a little insinuation
of pink in the azalea, coiled
garden hoses slackening on the lawn—
our orchestra has practiced
violence on the latest anthem to spring.
Fingers blistering, eyes bleared by sweat,
they're having to do it with feeling, they're having
to torment beauty into being.

The Fidgeting

Easy to make prayers to the darkness, to break bread
with the inconceivable. Harder to love

the moon—dusty dead-white relic
in the star museum, bald and obvious

as a drunken uncle. Hard to find worth
in the crooked pine that creaks

outside the kitchen window, every twig
a wagging finger as it lectures

on the miracle of the physical world.
Any day is the same day—the hours

writhe like worms in a bucket.
One can be an astonished infant

for only so long before the fidgeting,
before a flock of blackbirds bursting

from poplars, or a sodden collection
of fallen leaves blown against a fence,

is wearisome. Even the stiff, bloated opossum
by the roadside is only a brief diversion

before one longs to follow the opossum-soul,
to know where it goes and how it fares

in the province it scuttles off to,
the who-knows-where, anywhere but here.

Got No Blues

Harry Lee Gervais, 1912–1998

My grandfather's mind is in his hat,
his hat is on a hook in the checkroom of the Trianon,
his shoe is at the edge of the dance floor, tapping,
his right hand is riveting an airplane's wing,
his left is wiping clean a soda fountain counter,
his tie is askew,
his needle is in the groove,
his left eye is peering through the windshield of a Packard,
his right is weeping for his dead brother,
his liver is giving up drink,
his heart is in the right place,
his fingers are on the saxophone keys,
his knees are in the flowerbed.

After the tongue slackened and detached from the brain
and the suit drooped on the bones, and he gave up
his Armstrong and Beiderbecke records to my collection,
death's rest was a bad cigar,

so his ear is pressed to the radio turned down low
while his wife reads a magazine,
his head moving again to the music,
an almost imperceptible steady yes.

Dumbwaiter to Heaven

The dead try their luck in the great star casino
and win on every throw. Their perfect skin
glistens as they mingle, admiring

each other's tuxedos and sequined gowns
while down here it's getting hard to see
beneath the laggard clouds, backlit and burnished.

It's getting hard to deliver this frozen fish
when the latch at the back of the truck
keeps coming unfastened, and last night's snow

blocks my route through the back roads. It's hard
to grip my clipboard in the cold, to fill
each order form in triplicate before the ink

clogs in my pen. Oh, to call in sick
and search through the farthest dark and feel
for the crank that works the dumbwaiter to heaven

and crawl in. Oh, to stow away and subsist
by letting some small sweet crumb
dissolve on the tongue. But one is lulled

by distractions—as, for instance, seated
in the cab of my idling truck, I'm trying
to reach this itch on my back, I'm trying

to work this ball and socket joint. I like
the way my breath makes brief puffs of steam
that drift and vanish. I like the sleet

that blurs the windshield, melting here and there
to a single drop that swells, then breaks
into a quick runnel, plunging down.

Where the Past Went

Farewell, fedoras for the men, farewell, furs for the ladies,
they're flung in a trunk, the trunk flung in the room
of what's long gone: rumble seats, slide rules, whiff
of a rose plucked in some forgotten summer,
so long to the popular song on the old Victrola,
to scraps of the past swept into shadows,

trapped in a musty room, door overgrown with ivy
and rusted shut, the busted Underwood is there
with its missing books on Burmese cooking, chattering
Teletypes, tin box of ribbon and string, the light as it looked
that day the sun went red before an August rain,
it's all there, it hasn't gone, it's not coming back,

dirt under Dad's nails, Dad in the dirt, dust
spun into the air by a truck you watched, through tears,
disappear up a hill, you were six years old, now
you're five, you stretch your arms before you—in one fist
the licorice bought with a nickel you earned
by being good, and in the other, the nickel, not yet spent.

Some Words from My Ghost

If he's speechless, I've taken his words.
Twice, he lost his sense of himself. I had it.

At night I roost in his hair
breathing little zeroes into his ear

then appear in his dream as rain
or a bee bumping at a window.

I hang in his closet, I sleep in his shoe,
I ride in his hat, I do handstands

on the lip of his wine glass
and leave no prints, although I long to.

When he sits in his chair like this, staring
at nothing, pencil tip tapping against a tooth,

I sometimes think he sees me
dangling like a bat from the ceiling fan.

He imagines I'll shudder into being
when a thumb shuts his eyelids at last,

but I crawled alongside him before he could walk,
I'm in his first communion photo

in the skinny shadow of his clip-on tie. Now
with his clouding eye, his beard gone silver,

with the loss of him haunting me already,
I make him feel me, I give him a twinge in his chest

when he glimpses a skittering leaf on pavement
or a girl's red cap in a passing school bus.

I love that catch in his breath,
that look he gets.

III

Erasure

Dusk. Low noise from the frog pond, each call
a small coffin weight.

                Some radiant unreason
beyond reach. Here,
then here. A few dogwood blossoms,
fallen already, burn
in the shadowy grass.

                Everything hinting
of elsewhere, of what was—some fact
the body took into itself
with fine inattention
at three years old, or seven, sweet
seed in the teeth the tongue can't get at.

Day's work shirt turned inside out,
unstitching—robed night approaching,
one wants to say. But

the steady erasure of light
is a lesson in error and revision. I've seen
enough dusks to say that. Enough
dusks, but not this one.

                In the half-dark, the firs
look turreted. Turquoise dragonfly
in the long-stemmed weeds. Then gone.

In the Very Temple of Delight, Veil'd Melancholy

At a hint you were happy, she'd want you
to picture a fistful of dirt
skimming across your coffin lid.

Joy was tragedy waiting to happen—
a candle flame wavering near the kitchen curtains,
a toddler forgotten at the edge of the pool.

When she called you down to the dock to gaze
at the twilit lake, you knew she'd glimpsed
the skeleton rowing his little skiff.

Then when, chilled, almost invisible
to each other in the dark, you turned to walk
back home, and she kissed you hard, she meant it.

Gouge, Adze, Rasp, Hammer

So this is what it's like when love
leaves, and one is disappointed
that the body and mind continue to exist,

exacting payment from each other,
engaging in stale rituals of desire,
and it would seem the best use of one's time

is not to stand for hours outside
her darkened house, drenched and chilled,
blinking into the slanting rain.

So this is what it's like to have to
practice amiability and learn
to say the orchard looks grand this evening

as the sun slips behind scumbled clouds
and the pears, mellowed to a golden-green,
glow like flames among the boughs.

It is now one claims there is comfort
in the constancy of nature, in the wind's way
of snatching dogwood blossoms from their branches,

scattering them in the dirt, in the slug's
sure, slow arrival to nowhere.
It is now one makes a show of praise

for the lilac that strains so hard to win
attention to its sweet inscrutability,
when one admires instead the lowly

gouge, adze, rasp, hammer—
fire-forged, blunt-syllabled things,
unthought of until a need exists:

a groove chiseled to a fixed width,
a roof sloped just so. It is now
one knows what it is to envy

the rivet, wrench, vise—whatever
works unburdened by memory and sight,
while high above the damp fields

flocks of swallows roil and dip,
and streams churn, thick with leaping salmon,
and the bee advances on the rose.

Keeping House Alone

Dawn: the sun again, laying
the backyard bare. A solitary robin
picks his way across the lawn,
finding nothing.

All morning my boots
loll their muddy tongues by the door
where I abandoned them yesterday
after sloshing in muck and slush, wiggling
a rotting fence post from the ground
like a loose tooth.

      Noon:
a patch of shade remains
between the house and hedge.

Old snow lies bunched like a wedding dress.

At dusk, the trembling spruce and alder
tease their long shadows together
in the neighbor's yard. I'm inside

straightening the bath towel on its hook,
fixing the dripping spigot, steeping tea,
marking with pencil a thought in a book,

waiting till the house shrouds
itself in darkness—the hour
I'll give my body over
to sleep, then flail and roll
toward the center of the bed
like a man on fire.

Crepuscular

As if I'd shrugged off the cloak of my loneliness
and slipped on the shirt of the chill, diminishing light,
and it warmed me, and the owl didn't flinch
when I perched on his blackening branch,
and the fox commended my stealth as we skulked
shoulder to shoulder through the shadowy grass,

and the skunk I joined on his rounds said nothing,
and I said nothing, mind on the hunt,
and I watched the rising moon and did not
think it an assertion about myself,
and I hitched a ride in the hearse of the wind,
brakes skirling as it neared night's mausoleum;

as if I were hardly here, some small thing
doing its work in the dark, thoughtless,
or wasting no thought, always moving,
not this sunlit still life: familiar
arrangement of fingers and wrists and knees
and teeth and bright human heart.

Failed Love Poem

I could say I'm writing to recount
my latest stare-down with the *Here-and-now*

as it crouched at the plate and *What's-to-come*
leaned on its bat in the on-deck circle,

but I can't stop thinking of the past,
and this prattling is just to kill the silence.

I could say the night is a dark wave
that lifts and sinks and floats me toward

the harbor of my deepest need,
but it's just that I stay up late these days.

I could say our failure—you, at last,
on one side of a continent, I on the other—

is only another house we built together
or the child we never had—

or claim whatever error led to our ruin
could not have been seen in a world

that only looks away and drums its fingers,
stumped by its own riddle. I could say

I'm arranging these words to break
some nameless reader's heart, not yours

or mine, or claim this change is not
our doing, it's like what's done

to someone in a book whose author wishes
to show the blunder in believing

anything is certain, anything can't be lost.
Or I could say that we erased us.

In poems, one wills oneself to witness
the truth, no matter the cost. Not this one.

Quiet Hours

The fine contraption of the inner ear:
triple mirror and trigger, gears,
dwarf bones like divining rods—

I would gum it up, toss in a tiny rag
and jam the machinery, for a minute, a day,
turn the hose on it, rust the ratchets.

The din the wall mice make, the scratching
branch on the roof, the lark on the chain link,
let them rest from my listening. And let me

not hear myself think, let me shush
the sleepless soprano in me with the silk dress,
the wee missionary with his Bible and bullhorn.

Let it quit: in the kitchen, garage, yard, where a wind-
nudged pinecone thumps softly onto the lawn,
another answer to a question I haven't asked.

A Nearer Distance

Spring, and I close the door to the whistling finch,
I shut the shade against the sun
to write a line
about the names of flowers and their operations;

glancing up from the book about
the Big End, I notice
nothing happening: no smoke and locusts, only me
in the mirror, holding the book in my hands;

impelled by dusk to think
of a youthful summer, a lake,
my sudden encounter with a bat, I fail
to hear the owl screeching.

It's time to live
at a nearer distance, to lie
naked in a field and feel the wind,
like a big dog, lick my face;

it's time to curl at nightfall
on the stubbly grass and feel
its scratching, to note the mosquito
as it lands on the back of my hand, then swat him;

it's time to watch the scattered stars
collect into the shape of a man
hunched above the page of the earth,
reading it, forgetting it, reading it again.

Deciduous

I call the maple disconsolate—
the way it turns jaundice-yellow, hurling
its leaves to the ground in a windy fit.

I've watched it through the window all morning,
feeling it draw my regard
away from and toward myself.

The maple's score is a dirge for organ and cello.
My score is not as I learned it.

I kissed her. I didn't think I'd do that.

The tree stands in drizzle, stripped and tense
as if it has something to say
and can't say it.

I've loved the sound of saying
it's a cave, a snug nothing, I inhabit—

but she may be traipsing through leaves
this moment on a nearby street
in those blue mud boots, that green coat,
and the maple has taken on a stoic look,
surrounded by all it has given up.

It is the darkest copper. Her hair, her eyes.

I should step outside.
I should let the various parts of me
fall on the lawn
where she'll happen upon them,
bend down, and gather the best of them
into her arms.

Getting There

Sky smudged gray, like a dust mop.
Driveway gleaming after midday rain.

Where sloth intersects with knowledge,
that's my train stop. Leaning back
in my chair, foot propped
on the porch railing, I'm getting there.
To my own garden I shall come.

Late winter light, strained, pallid,
dragging something weighty behind it.

A bird struts on the neighbor's roof.
On the drainpipe, dents flecked with rust.

There are words like pebbles to mark one's way.
There are words like splinters
of ice on the tongue—they're gone.
There are words carved from white fire;
the smoke twists heavenward.

If I could stop looking, I would.
Or look without talking.
Nothing without its bit of beauty,
I know that, nothing to disagree with.

Not even night, approaching already
in pieces, fluttering. No, it's black snow.

The Coast of Oklahoma

Oh to stroll the Oklahoma coast
now that the hollyhock is in bloom and my love has returned
and her hair's in my tub
and her smudged socks clutter the bedroom floor
and her Subaru leaks its indiscreet spot
of oil in the driveway. All my ripe desire
is plucked—I'm left to think
of what cannot be had and feel its lack
like an intoxicant. Oh to pack
a big picnic and explore
the brackish shallow tidepools
of the Tulsa Gulf, where the skittery sandpiper
makes his earnest rounds, and gulls
wheel and pivot overhead, where after a rain
the waves are grayish-blue
and the jagged Alps of Iowa rise
in the north like a kept promise. I miss
already that pebbled stretch of sand
I've yet to see, my love
hunched against some salty gust
as she tests the water with a naked foot. O
Oklahoma shore, the mere thought of you
is enough to render charmless
the Hanging Gardens of Utah
and shame Orlando's grand canals.

My Gospel Is

I take my orders from the whiff
of the biscuit factory, the oily smell
of the bicycle repair shop.

I have caught myself in prayer,
nose lowered, longing
for the opposite side of the river,

for those white woods I've heard about
where one lets go at last the body's grip
and lifts, pale with knowledge, to hover

wingless in the windless air.
But I recover. A neighbor's cutting
lumber, loosing the pine plank's scent,

or a breeze is steeped in the stink
of marsh muck. My gospel is
the rolled-up rug discarded in a yard

and rained on, the fusty garden shed,
and the raised glass that stalls halfway
to the lips, the sweet milk gone bad.

Beside Myself

Dusk settles its loose garment
on the spruce, the low slope of straggling vines.

In the ash, a crow stops to pick his wing feathers
and vanishes. All afternoon I've felt nudged

as if the day were a series of subordinate clauses
leading to an unknown subject. For once

I am going to sit in the dark
and not take the dark as a symbol.

I am going to let a cloud crawl over the moon,
listen to the muskrat splash,

the possum grub in the underbrush,
and not feel blessed or penitent.

I will be a kind of sleep. It will mean
giving back the names of things.

Summary and Invocation

The moon mouthing its own name,
the stars tracing on the sky's slate all night,
the lake in a trance,
the sudden heavy rain that believes in the laying on of hands,
and the finch in the jack pine.

The wind fumbling at everything's buttons,
the brook working to tie itself into a half-hitch,
the June peaks tipped with snow, a pentimento of winter—
part of the world's incoherent letter, addressed to no one,
    therefore useless and beautiful.
And the finch in the jack pine.

NOTES

Page 9: The title "The Very Button" is from *Hamlet*, 2.2. References in the first stanza are to *Othello*, 2.2; *Wuthering Heights*; and *Hamlet*, 2.2.

Page 33: The title "It Rusts Iron and Ripens Corn" is taken from Walter Pater's *The Renaissance.*

Page 42: "Got No Blues" is the title of a recording by Louis Armstrong and His Hot Five.

Page 50: The title "In the Very Temple of Delight, Veil'd Melancholy" is taken from Keats's "Ode on Melancholy."

A NOTE ON THE AUTHOR

Chris Forhan was raised in Seattle and educated at Washington State University (B.A.), the University of New Hampshire (M.A.), and the University of Virginia (M.F.A.). His first book, *Forgive Us Our Happiness*, won the Bakeless Prize. He has also published two chapbooks, *x* and *Crumbs of Bread*. His poetry has won a Pushcart Prize and has appeared in *Poetry, Ploughshares, New England Review, Parnassus*, and other magazines. He teaches at Auburn University and in the Warren Wilson M.F.A. Program.

A NOTE ON THE PRIZE

The Samuel French Morse Poetry Prize was established in 1983 by the Northeastern University Department of English in order to honor Professor Morse's distinguished career as teacher, scholar, and poet. The members of the prize committee are Francis C. Blessington, Joseph deRoche, Victor Howes, Stuart Peterfreund, Guy Rotella, and Ellen Scharfenberg.